THE G.I. SERIES

Distant
Thunder

Left: An Artilleryman of Battery H, 1st United States Artillery dressed in his 1883-pattern fatigue blouse and wearing an 1874-pattern US belt plate at the time of the Spanish-American War. Note the 1895-pattern forage cap and insignia with regimental and battery designations. (NPS)

THE G.I. SERIES

THE ILLUSTRATED HISTORY OF THE AMERICAN SOLDIER, HIS UNIFORM AND HIS EQUIPMENT

Distant Thunder

The U.S. Artillery from the Spanish-American War to the Present

Alejandro M. de Quesada

Greenhill Books
LONDON

Stackpole Books
PENNSYLVANIA

Greenhill Books

British Library Cataloguing in Publication Data

Quesada, Alejandro M. de
Distant thunder: the US Artillery from the Spanish-American
War to the present. – (The G.I. series: the illustrated history
of the American soldier, his uniform and his equipment;
v.26)
1. United States. Army–Artillery 2. United States.
Army–Artillery–History 3. United States.
Army–Artillery–Uniforms
I. Title
355.8'21'0973

ISBN 1-85367-464-8

Library of Congress Cataloging-in-Publication Data available

ABBREVIATIONS

ADEQHR	ADEQ Historical Resources, Inc. Collection
AMQ	Photos by A.M. de Quesada
FtM	Fort Morgan State Park, AL
NA	National Archives, College Park, MD
NPS	National Park Service, Gulf Islands National Seashore
PAO24ID	Public Affairs Office, 24th Infantry Division
RGB	Robert G. Borrell, Sr. Collection
USA	United States Army

ACKNOWLEDGEMENTS

I would like to thank the following individuals, organizations,
and institutions that made this work possible: John Phillip
Langellier; George Pappas, Colonel, USA (Ret.); Robert G.
Borrell, Sr.; A. M. de Quesada, M.D.; National Archives, College
Park, MD; National Park Service, Gulf Islands National
Seashore, Gulf Breeze, FL; The Casemate Museum, Fortress
Monroe, VA; Fort Morgan State Park, AL; U.S. Army Military
History Institute, Washington, D.C.; U.S. Army Quartermaster
Museum, Fort Lee, VA; U.S. Army Ordnance Museum,
Aberdeen Proving Ground, MD; Public Affairs Office, 24th
Infantry (Mechanized) Division (prior to inactivation in 1996
and reactivation in 1999); Fort Stewart Museum (formerly
known as the Victory Museum), Fort Stewart, GA; 116th Field
Artillery Regiment, Fl National Guard; 265th Air Defense
Artillery Regiment, Fl National Guard; Camp Blanding
Museum, Starke, FL; ADEQ Historical Resources, Inc.; and,
sincere gratitude to the members of The Company of Military
Historians for their guidance and camaraderie.

Design and layout by David Gibbons and Anthony A. Evans,
DAG Publications Ltd
Edited by Andy Oppenheimer
Printed in China

DISTANT THUNDER
THE U.S. ARTILLERY FROM THE SPANISH–AMERICAN WAR TO THE PRESENT

The end of the Spanish-American War helped propel the United States onto the world stage as an imperial power with the acquisition of Puerto Rico, Guam, Hawaii, and the Philippine Islands. With the build-up of a modern navy and coastal defenses, the army still appeared to be using the same equipment and uniforms since the campaign against the American Indian in the West. At the onset of the 20th century the army was still using the M1885 3.2-inch field gun.

The field gun was developed in the mid 1880s but not produced in large numbers until the Spanish-American War. These pieces were used in Cuba, Puerto Rico, and the Phillipines. After 1897 the older guns of this model were modified by reducing the chamber volume drastically for an early variety of smokeless powder. Carriages were made of steel, with unique brakes that also served to dampen recoil and provide counter-recoil. Under some conditions the counter-recoil can be greater that the recoil, which moves the gun too far forward, earned it the nickname 'grasshopper'.

The coastal defenses of the United States were a different story. President Cleveland appointed a joint military/civilian board headed by Secretary of War, William C. Endicott, to evaluate proposals for new defenses in 1885. The board recommended a massive build-up of defenses along the coastline of the United States at a cost of $127 million. Congress created the Board of Ordnance and Fortification in 1888. Newly designed breech-loading guns and mortars were emplaced in concrete batteries containing underground magazines, and were constructed in such a manner that these emplacements blended in with their surroundings. A major feature of these defenses was the creation of electrically controlled minefields. Many of the concrete coastal fortifications that still exist are referred to as Endicott-era fortifications.

On 3 March 1902, General Orders Number 52 separated the coast from field artillery as separate branches of the army. The insignia specified for each branch was a large projectile in the red oval over crossed cannons to represent the coast artillery. The short-lived caisson wheel in the red oval over crossed cannons represented field artillery. Advanced artillery education in these fields was necessary. The artillery school at Fort Monroe in Virginia formed a part of a developing army-wide system of military education. Soon other schools offering specific courses such as the School of Submarine Defense at Fort Totten and the School of Application for Cavalry and Field Artillery at Fort Riley were being established. The field artillery school that began as a practical course of conduct of fire was set up at Fort Sill, Oklahoma.

With the disappearance of the frontier, the mission of Fort Sill gradually changed from cavalry to field artillery. The first artillery battery arrived at Fort Sill in 1902 and the last cavalry regiment departed in May 1907. The School of Fire for the Field Artillery was founded at Fort Sill in 1911 and continues to operate today as the world-renowned U.S. Army Field Artillery School. At various times Fort Sill has also served as home to the Infantry school of Musketry, the School for Aerial Observers, the Air Service Flying School, and the Army Aviation School. Today as the U.S. Army Field Artillery Center, Fort Sill remains the only active Army installation of all the forts on the South Plains built during the Indian wars.

In the years leading up to World War I, the army had introduced the Model 1902-05 3-inch field gun. The 3-inch field gun was the first American field gun to use a recoil-absorbing carriage in the modern sense. It had a hydraulic buffer with a coil spring for counter-recoil. The carriage remained the same throughout its production years, until 1916. The gun tube changed slightly in 1904 and 1905. These pieces were used in the Pancho Villa Expedition, but not fired in action. They were kept in the United

States for training during World War I and not sent overseas. They continued in limited use for training until the 1930s, to use up old ammunition stocks. Most were converted to salute guns by cutting a groove in the chamber and fitting a choke ring which will only accept a short blank cartridge.

In World War I, the airplane became a formidable new attack weapon. Recognizing this new threat, the Secretary of War ordered three Coast Artillery Corps officers to Europe in July 1917 to study French and English anti-aircraft techniques. This study led to the establishment of the American Anti-aircraft School at Langres, France on October 10, 1917. Meanwhile, an urgent request by General Pershing that anti-aircraft units be formed for immediate service in France resulted in America's first anti-aircraft battalion being activated in November 1917. Units of this battalion began arriving at the French anti-aircraft school in December, where they studied the French 75-millimetre (mm) cannon modified for anti-aircraft use.

The versatile French model 75-mm field gun of 1897 was adopted in 1917 for use by American forces in France. Its date designation relates to the original French model year when it was put into service as the most advanced field gun of its time. It was the first to use a hydro-pneumatic recuperator which remains much the same today. It was the standard divisional artillery piece in the U.S. Army until replaced by the 105-mm howitzer at the outbreak of World War II. During the 1930s various carriage modifications adapted it to rubber tires and provided high-angle fire. The vast majority of French 75s were modified for World War II use, including mounting on half tracks and submarines.

By September 1939 a large portion of the coast artillery was anti-aircraft in nature, and as the threat of enemy invasion faded, coast artillery personnel and assets were increasingly transformed into anti-aircraft artillery units. Anti-aircraft Artillery (AAA) was officially separated from coast artillery on March 9, 1942. AAA played a major role in World War II. With its arsenal of air defense weapons, which included the 3-inch, 90-mm, 40-mm, 37-mm guns and the .50-caliber machine-guns, anti-aircraft artillerymen were among the first units to be shipped to the Pacific theater. They participated in the landings of North Africa and the invasion of Europe that followed.

The AAA played a major role in all theaters of World War II, particularly in the aerial defense of Antwerp. AAA units had destroyed 97.8 percent of all V-1s approaching Antwerp, eliminating 89 out of 91 of the flying bombs. The Belgian army conferred the coveted Fourragère upon the members of the American AAA units involved in the defense, with the following citation of two which read:

"The units of the Antwerp X Anti-aircraft Artillery Command played a heroic part in the organization and maintenance of the anti-aircraft defense, with a view of opening the Antwerp Port on 28 November 1944. They caused the failure of the supreme attack of V-1 bombs thrown by the Germans located in the Trier area, as well as of the areas situated at the northwest of Nimegue. Due to the unceasing efforts of the personnel belonging to these units, the materiel destruction and loss of lives for the Belgian civilians as well as for the Allied troops was held to the minimum. Fighting day and night, these military personnel performed their duty in a remarkable way. This resulted in the liberation of the harbor of Antwerp and the forwarding of supplies and ammunition to five Allied armies. The heroic behavior of these units honors very much the Antwerp X Anti-aircraft Artillery Command and the Allied forces."

In 1941, the 155-mm howitzer M1 went into production. During World War II this proved to be one of the best field artillery weapons of its class. The U.S. Army stopped using the 4.5-inch Gun M1 at the end of the war and eventually rebarreled many of them as 155-mm howitzers. The 155-mm howitzer M1 was retained long after World War II.

Introduction of V1 and V2 rockets in the latter part of World War II marked the beginning of the guided-missile era and the end of fixed coastal fortifications. By 1950, almost all of the big coastal guns were scrapped, all the harbor defense commands dismantled, and old coast defense reservations were either converted to other uses by the government or declared surplus. The Army Reorganization Act of 1950 abolished the coast artillery corps as a separate branch of the army.

During the Korean War, General Matthew B. Ridgway stated "Artillery has been and remains the great killer of communists. It remains the great saver of soldiers, American and Allied. There is a direct correlation between piles of shells and piles of corpses. The bigger the former, the smaller the latter". Several factors were responsible for the important role artillery assumed in the Korean War and for the influence of ammunition requirements on the war's conduct. Rapid maneuver during the opening months of the conflict soon gave way to stalemate, somewhat like that experienced in World War I. As a result, during the last two years of the

Korean War, while the truce talks at Panmunjom progressed at a glacial pace, U.S. commanders relied on artillery to do the lion's share of the fighting: interdicting enemy movements, responding to enemy batteries, and countering enemy offensive actions. The beginning of the truce talks led to a change in battlefield tactics, with the artillery barrage replacing the hill assault as the primary battlefield activity. The number of artillery pieces increased during the course of the war, which, of course, led to greater demands for ammunition.

The United Nations' (UN) forces used three basic calibers of artillery during the Korean War: 105-mm, 155-mm, and 8-inch. However, the artillery rounds did not come completely assembled. The 155-mm and 8-inch howitzers fired separate-loading ammunition, which was composed of four separate components: primer, propellant, projectile, and fuse. Components were issued and delivered separately, which created a logistics nightmare. The 105-mm howitzers in the UN inventory fired semi-fixed ammunition; propellant was divided into increments, or charges, and the charges were tied together and stored in cartridge cases. Each howitzer crew adjusted the charge by lifting the projectile from its case, removing increments not required, and returning the projectile to the case. The forces in the field also required several different ammunition types.

Depending on the tactical situation, maneuver commanders could call for smoke, illumination, or high-explosive ammunition, and each type required a different shell-and-fuse combination. The average 155-mm round, fully assembled, weighed almost 100 pounds. The standard 105-mm projectile weighed half that, and the 8-inch round weighed an average of 198 pounds. Thus, delivery of artillery rounds required a significant lift capability in terms of both weight and volume.

From July 15, 1950 to July 27, 1953, the 15th Field Artillery Battalion (Bn) established two records unequaled by any other artillery unit during the Korean War. In one 24-hour period during the battle for Bloody Ridge, the 15th FA Bn fired 14,425 rounds. Additionally, from August 26 through September 2, 1951, in support of the 2nd ID during the battle of Heartbreak Ridge, the 15th FA Bn fired 69,956 rounds. For its actions during its three continuous years in some of the bloodiest fighting of the war, the 15th FA Bn was awarded 10 campaign streamers.

Although enemy aircraft were not a significant factor in the Korea and Vietnam wars, air defenders contributed in numerous ways as part of the combined arms team. On June 20, 1968, Air Defense Artillery (ADA) was created as a basic branch of the army in General Orders Number 25, dated June 14, 1968.

During the war in Vietnam, numerous ADA and field artillery units participated in the conflict. One unit, the 7th Bn, 15th Field Artillery, held an honorable record while serving in Vietnam from 1967 to 1971. At that time the 7th Bn, 15th Arty was armed with 8-inch self-propelled howitzers, later re-tubed for 175mm. After an intensive period of unit training and equipment maintenance, the Indianheads of the 7th Bn, 15th Arty deployed to Vietnam on board the S.S. Walker in early June 1967. Landing at Qui Nhon, South Vietnam on July 1, 1967, the Battalion was assigned to the 41st Arty Group, First Field Forces Vietnam (IFFV). During the Battalion's four years and four months in Vietnam, the Indianheads of the Fighting Fifteenth fired over 360,000 rounds of deadly and accurate heavy artillery fire, were credited with 850 enemy killed by artillery, destroyed over 1,200 reinforced bunkers, and destroyed numerous other hard targets. The Fighting Fifteenth was awarded a total of 13 streamers to add to its unit colors for the following campaigns: Counteroffensive, Phase III; Tet Counteroffensive; Counteroffensive, Phase IV; Counteroffensive, Phase V; Counteroffensive, Phase VI; Tet 69/Counteroffensive; summer-fall 1969; winter-spring 1970; Sanctuary Counteroffensive; Counteroffensive, Phase VII; Consolidation I; Consolidation II; and the Cease Fire. Additionally, the Indianheads of the Fighting Fifteenth were awarded the Republic of Vietnam Cross of Gallantry w/Palm streamer, embroidered VIETNAM 1967-1971.

On a human level, individuals, not artillery, are the real heroes. On 17 October 1967, 2nd Lt. Harold B. Durham, Jr. distinguished himself by conspicuous gallantry while assigned to Battery C, 6th Battalion, 15th Artillery. 2nd Lt. Durham was serving as a forward observer with Company D, 2nd Battalion, 28th Infantry during a battalion reconnaissance-in-force mission. 2nd Lt. Durham's gallant actions in close combat earned him the Congressional Medal of Honor, but cost him his life. On July 28, 2000, the 2nd Bn, 15th FAR, located at Fort Drum, NY, dedicated their Headquarters Building as 'Durham Hall' in honor of 2nd Lt. Harold 'Pinky' Durham. Additionally, an M102, 105-mm howitzer was named 'pinky' in his honor complete with 6th Bn, 15th FA bumper markings.

A technological revolution of sorts impacted on artillery in the 1980s. Korean War-era technology was replaced with push-button warfare and the pinpoint accuracy of today's artillery. The deadly precision of the M109A6 Paladin howitzer and the destructive potential of the multiple launch rocket system (MLRS) require less ammunition logistics support than artillery did in previous wars. Nonetheless, accuracy does not necessarily mitigate ammunition needs. With two howitzer battalions and one MLRS battalion currently stationed in Korea, the Army clearly will have to do more with less.

The Iraqi invasion of Kuwait during the early morning hours of August 2, 1990 initiated a chain of events leading to the largest deployment and subsequent combat use of Army missiles in U.S. history. Backed by the UN as well as the combined might of a 28-member coalition, the United States drew a 'line in the sand' in defense of Saudi Arabia and for the liberation of Kuwait.

During Operation Desert Shield/Storm virtually every one of the Army's fielded missile systems managed and supported at Redstone Arsenal were sent to Southwest Asia (SWA). Three general types of missiles were deployed: air defense (Avenger, Chaparral, Stinger, Hawk, and Patriot); anti-armor (Dragon, TOW [tube-launched, optically-tracked, wire-guided], Hellfire, and Shillelagh); and artillery (Hydra-70, MLRS, and the Army TACMS [army tactical missile system]). Of these systems Patriot, Dragon, Hellfire, Hydra-70, MLRS, TOW, and the Army TACMS were fired in combat. The lack of targets was the primary reason that most of the air defense systems were not employed.

The U.S. Army Missile Command (MICOM) also supported other systems such as the ground/vehicle laser locator designator (G/VLLD), the mast mounted sight (MMS), the M-901 improved TOW vehicle (ITV), the forward area alerting radar (FAAR), and various night sights that provided coalition forces with a night-fighting capability not available to the opposing Iraqi army. Operation Desert Storm provided a unique opportunity to see how well the Army's inventory of advanced weapons functioned in actual combat conditions.

On January 18, 1991, Iraq fires the first Scud missiles at Israel and Saudi Arabia. Battery A, 2d Battalion, 7th ADA, 11th ADA Brigade scores the first combat kill for the Patriot system after successfully intercepting the first Scud over Dhahran, Saudi Arabia. A Battery, 6th Battalion, 27th Field Artillery, attached to VII Corps, fired the first two Army TACMS missiles of Operation Desert Storm in counterattacks against Iraqi artillery at the Kuwaiti border firing on Saudi Arabia. These were the first rounds fired in anger by VII Corps since World War II, as well as the first fired by U.S. Army field artillery in the Persian Gulf War.

An advance party teams consisting of elements from the 41st Field Artillery Brigade entered Iraq and began preparing gun positions on February 23, 1991. On February 24, VII Corp artillery shot a massive artillery prep that would further soften Iraqi forces and clear the way for advancing VII Corps armored divisions. Joining 3rd Armored Division in support of 4/32nd Armor, 2/82nd FA (who, in turn, was support for 4/67 Armor) and 4/82nd FA traveled north into Iraq encountering small pockets of resistance until February 27-28, and where the 41st Artillery Brigade encountered two Iraqi Republican Guard Divisions (Tawakalna and Medina). They were supported by elements of the Iraqi 52nd Armored Division and 17th Armored Division. After sixteen hours of fighting, giving credit to superior training, leadership, and supplies, the Americans were victorious – with light casualties and maintaining high morale. Overall, the brigade – supporting four different divisions (1st Calvary, 1st Infantry Division, 101st Airborne, and 3rd Armored Division) – had fired over 5,440 artillery shells and 1,286 MLRS rockets. Heading east into Kuwait, the Artillery Brigade stood guard against any further Iraqi aggression and returned home at the beginning of May 1991.

Beginning at the end of the Spanish-American War in 1898 to the end of the millennium, a century of advanced developments within the artillery are very much in evidence. From its meager beginnings in France during World War I, Air defense artillery has evolved from crude field pieces to highly sophisticated and exceptionally accurate missile and gun systems. Evolving technology subsequently produced the Hawk, Safeguard's Spartan and Sprint, Chaparral, Redeye, Stinger, Hawk, and Patriot. This technological prowess defeated the Scud ballistic missile threat in the Gulf War and is now fielding the theater high-altitude area air defense (THAAD) system. The 15th Field Artillery Battalion's expenditures of ammunition in 1951 are unthinkable today. With the deadly precision of the M109A6 Paladin howitzer and the destructive potential of the multiple launch rocket system artillery requires less ammunition logistics support than in previous wars. Even in the Gulf War, howitzer battalions fired nothing close to the 15,000 rounds a day fired by the 15th FA in Korea.

Above: The United States Army came into the 20th century wearing the same uniform and equipage used during the Indian campaigns in the American West and the war with Spain. The artillerymen preparing to fire their M1885 3.2-inch field gun are seen wearing the drab 1889-pattern campaign hat, the dark blue 1883-pattern campaign shirt, khaki trousers, and leggings. (ADEQHR)

Right: In 1902 the artillery branch was divided into two distinct components: coast artillery and field artillery. These coast artillerymen are seen wearing the new dress uniform adopted by the army. Note the M1840 NCO Sword worn by the electrician sergeant on the right. (ADEQHR)

Right: The field artillery wore much of the same uniform as their counterparts with only minor differences in the insignia used. The stable sergeant on the far right is wearing the M1840 light artillery saber. Note the field artillery guidon in the background; the coast artillery utilized a projectile within crossed cannons. (ADEQHR)

Left: After the war with Spain, the U.S. Army adopted a new field uniform in 1902. The old campaign hat was retained with the olive-drab service uniform. Note the issuance of the .38 Colt and leather cartridge cases to the NCOs. Of particular interest is the OD version of the 1902 dress cap and the use of campaign ribbons. (ADEQHR)

Left: This print created by Henry Ogden shows a commanding brigadier general inspecting a post with the key members of his staff and line officers standing by. Many officers are seen still utilizing the M1895 Officers undress coat with its distinctive mohair braid along the front and collar of the uniform. (ADEQHR)

Right: A major-general and officers of the line and staff corps wearing their special uniform for evening wear-mess jacket. The outstanding feature of the lieutenant-colonel of Artillery's uniform is the red lapels and the crossed cannon insignia on his sleeves, signifying his service. (ADEQHR)

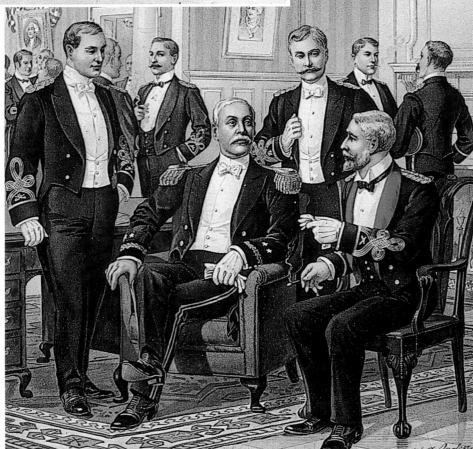

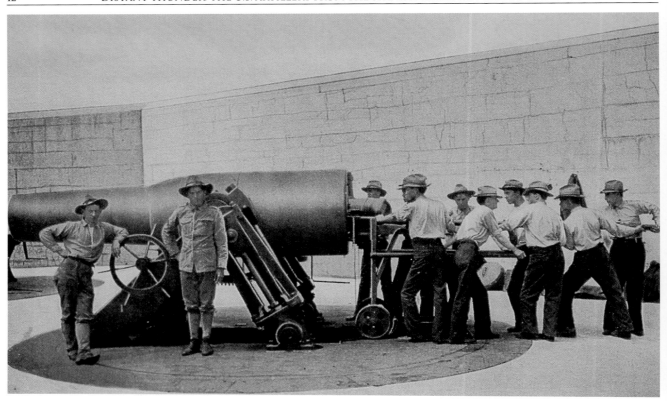

Above: A gun crew is seen loading a Model 1890 12-inch mortar in a seacoast fortification. The campaign hats are standard dress for all. The two artillerymen are seen wearing their olive-drab service uniforms while the other soldiers have piled up their coats along the wall of the gun pit. (ADEQHR)

Below: A group photograph of members from the 10th Company Coast Artillery Corps in the Presidio of San Francisco, circa 1907. Note the use of the 1902 dress cap with the M1883 sack coat. These Indian War vintage coats were issued to the Coast Artillery until stocks were depleted in 1914! (ADEQHR)

Above: Artillerymen preparing their M1902 3-inch field gun for transportation. In 1910 the 'Montana Peak' campaign hat and new olive-drab wool and cotton field uniforms were introduced. In time the service uniform relegated the 'dress blues' to special functions. (ADEQHR)

Below: The French M1897 75-mm field gun was adopted by the American Expeditionary Forces in 1917. From World War I, this was the standard divisional artillery piece in the U.S. Army until replaced by the 105-mm howitzer at the outbreak of World War II. This early 1930s image shows artillerymen wearing the 'Montana Peak' campaign hat, olive-drab wool pants, khaki shirts, and leggings. (ADEQHR)

Above: Gun crew using a M3 37-mm antitank gun in the early part of World War II. All are wearing the overseas caps, M1941 olive-drab field jackets, olive-drab M1937 trousers, and canvas leggings. (ADEQHR)

Below: A 105-mm howitzer crew in Vietnam, circa 1968. The soldier in the white undershirt is seen wearing tropical combat trousers while the others are wearing utility uniform shirts and trousers. All are using the M1 'steel pot' helmet issued by the United States Army since World War II. (VMU)

Above: Full dress uniform of a colonel of artillery. The distinctive red trim is the color of the artillery. This dress uniform has changed little since World War II and is still in use today for special occasions only. (AMQ)

Right: Not much has changed in the mess dress uniform that Henry Ogden illustrated in the early part of the 20th century, as worn by Colonel George Pappas of the Air Defense Artillery in 1998. Note the distinctive red lapels of his jacket and the ADA metal insignia on his sleeves. Before the 1970s, branch of service insignia were often embroidered, whereas after 1974 they were in metal. The medals he is wearing are for past services as president with The Company of Military Historians. (AMQ)

Right: Colonel George Pappas in his white mess dress uniform in 2000. Clearly visible is the ADA metal insignia on his sleeve. Col. Pappas began his military career with the Coast Artillery Corps before World War II and saw the changes when the anti-aircraft artillery was separated from the CAC, including the disbandment of the CAC and the AAA becoming the Air Defense Artillery in 1968. (AMQ)

Below: Members of the 116th Field Artillery Regiment of the Fl National Guard are seen preparing a 105-mm howitzer for transportation in 2000. The battle dress uniform (BDU) was introduced in the years following Vietnam and is now the current everyday work uniform for the Army and for the other branches of the armed services. (AMQ)

NO 183
5 INCH RIFLE

Top: On to Cuba! This individual is dressed in a M1889 campaign hat, 1883-pattern campaign shirt, khaki trousers, and canvas leggings. He is armed with either a .45 Colt Artillery Model Revolver or a .38 Colt Army revolver in his brown leather holster. He is seated upon a 5-inch siege gun. (ADEQHR)

Right: Artillery Sergeant William Gard of the garrison of Presidio in San Francisco is seen in his garrison uniform. Notice the 1872-pattern chevrons on his blouse and the one-inch red stripe on his trousers. (ADEQHR)

Above: A close-up view of the 1902 dress uniform worn by a member of the 151st Coast Artillery Company. Interesting uniform features are the placement of the metal insignia and the arrangement of the aiguillette. The circular patch on his sleeve is a 1st Class Gunners rating. (RGB)

Left: In 1902 new changes were made in the uniforms of the U.S. Army. This coast artillery bugler of the 43rd Coast Artillery Company is wearing the new pattern dress uniform. The two narrow red stripes on the trousers designate his rank as a lance corporal. (RGB)

Left: The 1902 uniform changes took several years to phase out the uniforms previously worn by the soldiers. This battery quartermaster sergeant is wearing the new 1902-pattern chevrons and Coast Artillery insignia on his 1899-pattern khaki uniform blouse. Everything else is Spanish-American War vintage, including the 1889-pattern campaign hat and the M1874 US belt plate. Of interest is the 2nd Class gunners rating on his sleeve and the 1886-pattern gauntlets. (ADEQHR)

Below: Two artillerymen wearing the new khaki service uniform adopted in 1902. The 1890-pattern summer helmets continued to be utilized for a short time after the uniform change. The use of branch-of-service collar discs and campaign ribbon being worn by the soldier on the left dates this photograph after 1907. (ADEQHR)

Disapearing Gun, Fort Pickens; Santa Rosa I near Pensacola Fla. P

Above: Coast artillerymen are seen loading a 12-inch disappearing gun at Battery Pensacola in Fort Pickens (Santa Rosa Island, Fl) in 1900. The men are all wearing the 1890-pattern summer helmets and brown fatigue uniforms. (NPS)

Left: An interesting portrait photograph of a coast artilleryman in his 1902 khaki service uniform. The soldier had placed his 1902 pattern Coast Artillery collar insignia as a cap ornament and replaced his collar with branch-of-service discs that were adopted in 1907. (ADEQHR)

Above: Coast artillerymen of the Fl State Troops posing with a 10-inch disappearing rifle of Battery Cullum-Sevier in Pensacola Harbor. (NPS)

Below: Four coast artillerymen on maneuvers in Fl, circa 1907. The style of canvas 'puttees' worn were probably manufactured by Rosenwasser Brothers of New York and were patented by the company on 25 June 1907. The men are armed with the Model 1903 Springfield that replaced the Krag-Jorgensen Rifle. (NPS)

Above: Members of the 42nd Coast Artillery Company posing with their officers, 1905. The officers are wearing the new uniforms prescribed in the 1902 changes, while the enlisted are still wearing the obsolescent 1883-pattern sack coat with the new 1902-pattern caps and insignia. (ADEQHR)

Below: Gun crews posing with Model 1890 12-inch mortars in an Endicott-era seacoast battery. The men are wearing the brown fatigue uniforms commonly used by coast artillerymen. By the 1920s these canvas uniforms were also being issued in blue denim. (ADEQHR)

Right: These men are posing with a 4.72-inch Armstrong rifle in Battery Van Swearingen, Pensacola Harbor, 1907. (NPS)

Below: An interesting and rare photograph showing the positions of a gun crew manning a seacoast artillery piece during loading. The piece is a 10-inch Breech Loading Rifle set on a Barbette Carriage. (ADEQHR)

Left: In 1910 the service and field uniform was modified from a fold-down to a standing collar, as worn by this corporal of the 116th Coast Artillery Company. (RGB)

Right: Another view of the 1910 uniform as worn by a private first-class gunner. (RGB)

Above: A good detail image of coast artillerymen in fatigue and service uniforms, posing with a 3-inch rapid fire gun in Boston Harbor, 1915. The corporal in center is wearing the 1910-pattern tunic and has a 1st gunner, mine company rating. The inset shows the badge in detail. (Photo-RGB; Inset-FtM)

Below: Guard Mount of the 59th Coast Artillery Company in Boston, 1915. The men are wearing the pre-World War I overcoat adopted in 1902. The front leading edge had a very pronounced curve which was less pronounced in overcoats manufactured by 1917 and was virtually straight-edged from 1918 onwards. All the enlisted men are wearing the M1907 winter cap. (RGB)

Above: American artillerymen firing their Model 1902 3-inch field gun during the Mexican border expedition in 1916. In 1910 the 'Montana Peak' campaign hat and new olive-drab wool and cotton field uniforms were introduced. (ADEQHR)

Below: Horsedrawn artillery in the years before World War I.

All the men appear to be wearing the olive-drab cotton shirt adopted in 1916. (ADEQHR)

Opposite page: A close-up of the shirts adopted in 1916. Note the various shades on the cotton and wool trousers worn by the soldiers. (ADEQHR)

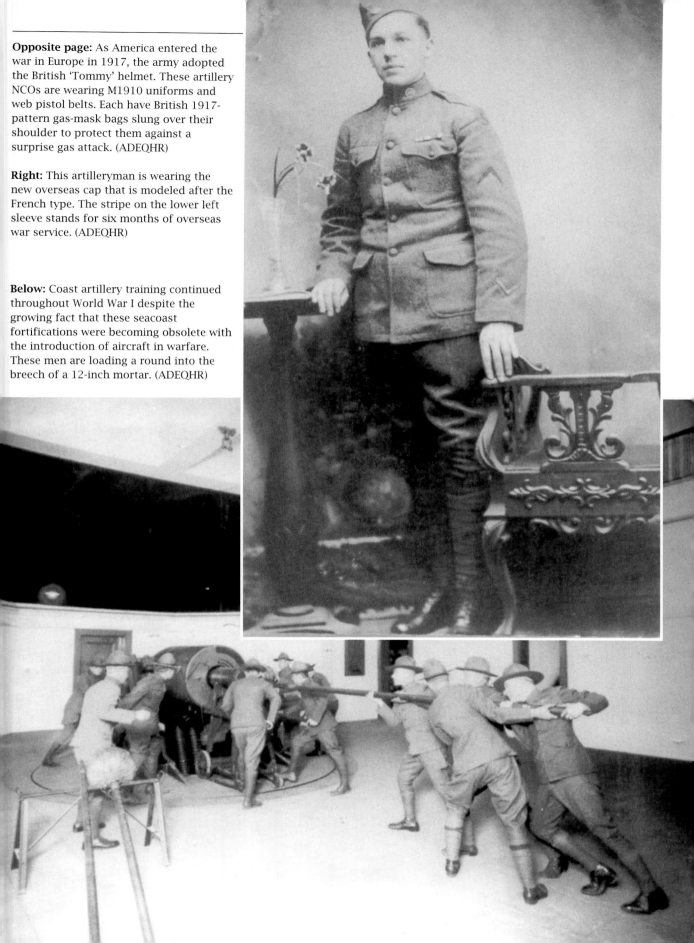

Opposite page: As America entered the war in Europe in 1917, the army adopted the British 'Tommy' helmet. These artillery NCOs are wearing M1910 uniforms and web pistol belts. Each have British 1917-pattern gas-mask bags slung over their shoulder to protect them against a surprise gas attack. (ADEQHR)

Right: This artilleryman is wearing the new overseas cap that is modeled after the French type. The stripe on the lower left sleeve stands for six months of overseas war service. (ADEQHR)

Below: Coast artillery training continued throughout World War I despite the growing fact that these seacoast fortifications were becoming obsolete with the introduction of aircraft in warfare. These men are loading a round into the breech of a 12-inch mortar. (ADEQHR)

Above: This 155-mm gun is being transported by tractors through Fortress Monroe Military Reservation during World War I. (ADEQHR)

Below: An American railway artillery piece being manned somewhere in France. Coveralls are worn by the gun crew on the gun platform, as are steel helmets and gas masks. (ADEQHR)

Above: A mobile Model 1918 3-inch anti-aircraft gun being pulled by a tractor. This gun remained a significant part of the army's arsenal until the beginning of World War II, especially for National Guard regiments. (ADEQHR)

Right: From the end of World War I (1918) to 1941, advances were made in detecting enemy aircraft and another entity was created within the Coast Artillery Corps to cover that role: the Anti-Aircraft Artillery (AAA). Shown here is a primitive aerial listening device being tested at Fortress Monroe, VA. (ADEQHR)

Above: Coast artillerymen await inspection of their weapons and kit in Hawaii during the 1920s. The use of khaki were widespread in tropical areas and in the southeastern U.S.A. The sergeant on the right has affixed his collar discs on his M1916 campaign shirt. (ADEQHR)

Below: Field artillerymen preparing to fire a 2.95-inch Vickers Sons and Maxim mountain gun. These guns were procured about 1900 and a few were used during the defense of the Philippines in 1941-1942. The distinctive insignia bearing the regimental crest on the campaign hats began to be used from 1924 on. (ADEQHR)

Above: Members of Battery E, 52nd Coast Artillery, gathered in front of an 8-inch gun mounted on a M1918 Barbette Carriage. The carriage was designed to be mounted on a railway car. The officers and men are wearing the new uniforms adopted in 1926. The uniform change gave the soldiers a totally different appearance and influences of this uniform continues to this day in one form or another. (ADEQHR)

Right: Colonel Homer W. Hesterly, commanding officer of the 116th Field Artillery Regiment, 1934: a fine close-up of an officer's M1926 tunic. Notice the new visored hat, the unit's distinctive insignia on his epaulettes, and the regimentally marked crossed cannons on his lapel. (ADEQHR)

Left: Lieutenant Colonel Byron E. Bushnell of the 56th Field Artillery Brigade. He is wearing the officer's overseas or garrison cap with gold/black trim. Of interest is the use of the distinctive insignia of the 56th Field Artillery Brigade on his cap and epaulettes. (ADEQHR)

Below: Fl National Guardsmen of the 116th Field Artillery Regiment are seen firing a French 75-mm gun. Note the wearing of the blue denim fatigue uniforms and the use of the 'Daisy Mae' caps. (ADEQHR)

Right: Brigadier General Sumter L. Lowry, Jr. commanding officer of the 56th Field Artillery Brigade. He has been known to wear his khaki garrison cap, his M1926 tunic with white shirt and black necktie, khaki trousers, and high laced cavalry boots – a popular style among high-ranking officers of the time. Note the distinctive insignia is also applied on the cap as well as on the epaulettes. (ADEQHR)

Below: A gun crew awaiting orders to fire their 8-inch railway artillery gun, 1935. All members are seen wearing the older brown canvas fatigue uniforms.

Opposite page, top:
Members of the 64th Anti-aircraft Artillery Battalion gathered around their M1928 3-inch AA gun in Hawaii. Notice the various styles and shades of the fatigue uniforms and the distinctive insignia worn on the campaign hats. (ADEQHR)

Right: An officer helps load a round of a French 75-mm field gun. The officer is wearing a khaki shirt with his OD wool pants, while the other enlisted men are wearing their OD wool winter shirt and trousers. The officer's garrison cap is adorned with the distinctive insignia of the 56th Field Artillery Brigade. (ADEQHR)

Opposite page, bottom: An interesting image showing men of the 64th AAA Battalion preparing to load a 3-inch AA gun. Of peculiar interest are the leather-trimmed khaki canvas leggings worn by the gun crew. (ADEQHR)

Below: The baseball team of the 64th Anti-aircraft Artillery Battalion, Hawaii, 1940. Many military units formed baseball teams to play against each other, including those from other branches of the armed services. The first sergeant (far left) and the sergeant (far right) are wearing the enlisted khaki uniform in garrison dress fashion with garrison cap and tucked-in necktie. (ADEQHR)

Opposite page: An enlisted man of the 517th Coast Artillery wearing his M1926 uniform and leather garrison belt. Note the coast artillery collar disc and unit distinctive insignia on his lapel. The patch is of the general headquarters reserve. (ADEQHR)

Above: Men from an anti-aircraft artillery unit manning a water-cooled .50 caliber Browning machine-gun after the Japanese attack in Pearl Harbor on December 7, 1941. The soldiers are all wearing the M1917A1 steel helmet and the soldier in the foreground is wearing a herringbone twill jacket while the others are wearing khaki shirts. (ADEQHR)

Below: The plotting room for Battery Worth in Fort Pickens, Florida during the early days of World War II. Next to the khaki uniforms the soldier in center is clearly wearing a bag for the M2A1-1-1 training gas mask. Campaign hats hang from the walls. (NPS)

Opposite page, top: A first sergeant of the Pensacola Harbor Defense is working at the battle board of a fire control station in Fort Pickens. He wears the enlisted man's winter service shirt in standard olive-drab shade 33 and necktie. The leather holster for his Colt Government Model .45 is suspended from a M1936 pistol belt. (NPS)

Below left: A river crossing for the crews of two 37-mm antitank guns during World War II. Noticeable is the M1 helmet that replaced the M1917A1 helmet in 1942. The men appear to be wearing herringbone twill (hbt) field caps and hbt uniforms, and are carrying M1 Garand rifles. (ADEQHR)

Right: An enlisted man from the Eastern Defense Command wearing a M1939 service coat. The coat differed slightly from the M1926 service coat with the addition of a bi-swing back and removal of the brass belt support hooks. (ADEQHR)

Below right: An artillery lieutenant from the 116th Field Artillery visiting family. He is wearing the M1939 officer's service coat and has omitted using the M1921 Sam Brown leather belt over his uniform's cloth belt. Another distinguishing feature of this officer's uniform was the addition of a strip of braid on the sleeves. (ADEQHR)

Left: A cook from Battery C, 160th Field Artillery Battalion, 45th Division is seen here making an American delicacy: glazed doughnuts. He is wearing the hbt field cap that had earflaps that could be pulled down, and a high-neck five-button sweater. (ADEQHR)

Below: Men from Battery C, 160th Field Artillery Battalion are enjoying a rare treat of glazed doughnuts. All are wearing the M1941 field jackets and winter service shirts. Other features are M-1937 wool trousers, M1943 hbt trousers, M1941 wool knit cap, M1 helmets, and an army-issue scarf. (ADEQHR)

Above: Soldiers from an AAA unit huddle close to a fire in a vain attempt to dry out during the rainy season somewhere in the Pacific. The trouserless soldier is wearing the M1943 field jacket while others are attempting to stay dry by wearing ponchos. The soldier on the far left is wearing the one-piece M1938 hbt suit. (ADEQHR)

Below: A 105-mm gun section from Battery C, 616th Field Artillery Pack Battalion, 10th Mountain Division, Italy 1945. All are wearing the armored force winter combat suit without the jackets. The cotton trousers were designed like overalls with a high front bib. (ADEQHR)

Left: An AAA unit's Bofors emplacement beside the 'Dragon's Teeth' in a captured segment of the Siegfried Line. (NA)

Right: An American 155-mm M2 heavy gun guards a beach on a Pacific atoll. Nicknamed the 'Long Tom', it kicked a 95-lb projectile upwards of 15 miles. (NA)

Left: An American 90-mm anti-aircraft gun overlooking a harbor on a remote Pacific island. Nearly all of the men are wearing the hbt trousers and M1 helmets. (NA)

Left: American artillerymen from the 84th Infantry Division test-fire a captured German 88-mm flak 36 gun. The standing soldiers are wearing the one-piece hbt suits while the seated soldier is wearing a M1943 field jacket. (NA)

Right: End of an era: a soldier squatting on a cut tube of a 12-inch seacoast gun at Battery Langdon, Fort Pickens, Florida, September 16, 1947. (NPS)

Right: In the latter part of World War II the 'Ike Jacket' was popularized by General Dwight 'Ike' Eisenhower to double as a battle and as a dress tunic. Both the 'Ike' and the M1939 service coat were worn throughout the 1950s. (ADEQHR)

Left: A 240-mm howitzer M1 being test-fired in a postwar demonstration. Nearly all are wearing the M1943 field jackets and M1 helmets. (NA)

Left: In the Korean conflict troops wore the M1951 field jacket, M1951 pile cap, and new field uniforms, as seen here. The two officers are wearing rubber arctic overshoes. (ADEQHR)

Right: Members of Battery A, 546th Field Artillery Battalion, gather for a photo, 1956. The soldiers are wearing the M1951 field cap that has been stiffened with cardboard or plastic inserts and are adorned with the unit's distinctive insignia. (ADEQHR)

Lower left: A soldier from the 71st Infantry Division Artillery taking a break, 1956. He is basically wearing World War II vintage equipment, consisting of the M1910 canteen with cover, the M1923 cartridge belt, the M1 (Garand) bayonet with M7 scabbard, the M1943 entrenching tool carrier, and the M1945 combat field pack. (ADEQHR)

Right: The utility uniform was introduced in the mid-1950s. For the first time a name tape and a tape with 'U.S. Army' were introduced to the uniform. The utility shirts were to be worn tucked in unless otherwise specified. Note the winter parka being worn by the soldier located third from the right. The chevron worn by the soldier on the far left is for a specialist third class which was re-changed to specialist four after 1959. (ADEQHR)

Above: A gun section working on a 155-mm howitzer M1, 1956. (ADEQHR)

Below: Crew of the 71st Infantry Division Artillery loading a 105-mm howitzer M2, 1956. (ADEQHR)

Above: Excellent view of the M1951 field jacket that differed slightly from the M1943 field jacket. Some of the soldiers are wearing M1936 pistol belts with M1942 first aid pouches, while the others are wearing M1923 cartridge belts. The soldier third from left is armed with an M3 'Grease' gun and the rest, with the M1 carbine. (ADEQHR)

Right: These artillerymen are displaying the widely used weapons in the years between World War II and the Vietnam War. The private first class on the left is holding the M1 Garand rifle while the sergeant on the right is holding a M1 carbine. (ADEQHR)

Left: Colonel John V. Roddy, commanding officer of the 71st Infantry Division Artillery, 1956. He is wearing the khaki summer service uniform prescribed for warm climates. Of interest is the placement of his rank and artillery insignia on the collar. The current serving 71st ID patch is sewn on the wearer's left sleeve while the past serving unit would be sewn on the wearer's right sleeve – as evidenced by the 3rd Infantry Division patch. Note the green felt 'Combat Leader' loops worn on the shirt's shoulder straps. (ADEQHR)

Top right: A battery of 8-inch howitzer M1s being paraded in Ft. Knox, Kentucky in the mid-1950s. This gun had a reputation for accuracy, and was in service after 1945, largely because it could handle firing a nuclear shell. This was one of the major artillery pieces used during the height of the Cold War. (ADEQHR)

Lower right: An artilleryman atop a 155-mm howitzer motor carriage M41. This self propelled gun was modified from a 155-mm Howitzer M1. The basic chassis is from a modified M24 light tank. These are still encountered from time to time in some National Guard units. (ADEQHR)

Left: In 1948 the army quartermaster wanted to decrease the size of chevron and make a distinction between soldiers serving in non-combat with those serving in combat units. Non-combat personnel wore small dark blue chevrons with gold designs and combat personnel wore the small gold chevrons with dark blue designs. After 1951 the chevrons were authorized for wear on the field uniforms. (ADEQHR)

Left: The army adopted the green service uniform on September 2, 1954, and it became available at quartermaster supply outlets two years later. After a permitted period for the older uniforms to be 'worn out', the green uniform became mandatory winter service attire in September 1961. The enlisted version is similar, but without the officer grade mohair braid on the sleeves and trousers. (ADEQHR)

Right: Specialist Four with the 1st Howitzer Battalion, 319th Artillery of the 82nd Airborne Division, is sighting his 106-mm recoilless rifle M40A1 during the Dominican Republic invasion in 1965. He is wearing his utility uniform and reversible camouflaged helmet cover over his M1C helmet. The M1C helmet is the airborne troops' version of the standard M1 and the additional web-straps of the M1C are in evidence. (ADEQHR)

Right: A major from the 265th Air Defense Artillery of the Fl National Guard wearing the new army green service uniform, 1966. The new uniform was made available in wool serge, gabardine, or polyester/wool blend. Though there are plans to change the service uniform, the green service uniform is still in use as of 2001. (ADEQHR)

Right: Three Fl Guardsmen during maneuvers in 1967. All are wearing the M1951 field jacket which is to be replaced by the M1965 field jacket by the end of the 1960s. The cap worn by the military policeman is a utility cap adopted in 1962. The soldier wearing the helmet liner is from the officer candidate school of the Fl National Guard. (ADEQHR)

Far left: A sergeant with the 1st Howitzer Battalion, 319th Artillery of the 82nd Airborne Division, is holding a fired round from one of the two captured rebel 105-mm Krupp howitzers used during the Dominican Republic invasion in 1965. He is carrying the M1956 pouches for the M14 magazines on his pistol belt.

Near left: Artillerymen loading a 203-mm howitzer self-propelled gun in Vietnam. Nearly all are wearing the tropical combat uniform or 'jungle fatigues' that came into use after 1963. There were variations of the uniform in olive green and camouflage. (U.S.A)

Below left: Firing a 105-mm howitzer in Vietnam. Note the army issued olive-green undershirt and the camouflaged covered M1 helmets of the soldiers. (U.S.A)

Right: The guidon for the 30th Air Defense Artillery (ADA) in an entrenched Vietnamese hill. On June 20, 1968, ADA was created out of the Anti-aircraft Artillery Battalion as a basic branch of the Army. (U.S.A)

Below: South Vietnamese artillerymen in action. The heavy American influence and involvement in the war can be clearly seen with the U.S.-issued equipment and uniforms. The only uniform difference in some cases from U.S. personnel would have been the insignia used by the South Vietnamese army. (U.S.A)

Left: The khaki shirts were continued until replaced by the olive-green shirts with slip-on rank sleeves for the epaulettes in the early 1980s. They were initially produced in cotton and later examples were of a similar cut in polyester-cotton perma-press fabric. This captain is with the 265th Air Defense Artillery, Fl National Guard, 1973. The ADA insignia was designed in 1957 and adopted the following year. (ADEQHR)

Below: These Fl Guardsmen from the 265th ADA are displaying a variety of equipment, uniforms and weapons. Of interest are the M16s fitted with the 40-mm M203 grenade launcher. (ADEQHR)

Right: Well into the early 1980s the utility uniform and M1 helmet continued to be used. (ADEQHR)

Above: The battle dress uniform (BDU) came into use in 1981 for all branches of the armed forces and is still in use as of 2001. The trainee firing the light antitank weapon (LAW) is wearing the M1965 field jacket. The woodland camouflage pattern gradually replaced the army olive green as the standard uniform appearance. (ADEQHR)

Left: Members from the ADA school wearing the olive-green M1965 field jackets over their BDUs. (ADEQHR)

A drill sergeant from the 1st ADA Training Brigade examines a recruit's M16 rifle, 1984. The old 'Montana Peak' campaign hat was retained by drill instructors as a symbolic sign that army traditions continue. (ADEQHR)

Above: A staff sergeant serving as courtesy patrol for the 1st ADA Training Brigade in Fort Bliss, TX, 1984. He is wearing the enlisted version of the army green service uniform. The five stripes on the wearer's lower left sleeve signified 15 years of service in the Army. (ADEQHR)

Top right: Members of the 1st Air Defense Artillery Training Brigade examining the workings of a M163 Vulcan. Based on the Gatling, this weapon had adjustable rates of fire whether it was being used for ground attack or anti-aircraft defence. The rate of fire was 1,180 rounds per minute. These weapons proved themselves against Iraqi aerial and land attacks during Desert Storm in 1991. (ADEQHR)

Right: Nicknamed the 'Battleking', a M109 of the 3rd Battalion, 41st Field Artillery fires off a round in Saudi Arabia during Operation Desert Shield/Storm. This self-propelled artillery vehicle is equipped with a 155-mm howitzer. (PAO24ID)

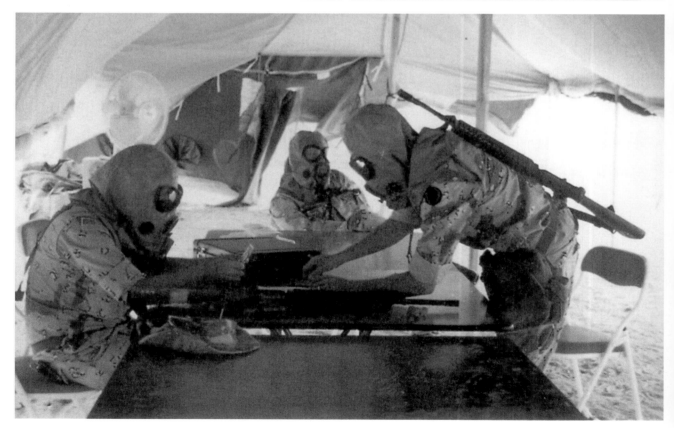

Top left: This crewman of a M163 Vulcan from the 1st Battalion, 5th Air Attack Artillery of the 24th Infantry Division looks more like an armored cavalryman than an artilleryman! He is wearing the DH-132 combat vehicle crewman's (CVC) helmet. (PAO24ID)

Left: Desert Shield/Storm, 1990/1991. The desert pattern BDUs were first introduced when U.S. troops were sent as part of the UN Multinational Force and Observers' mission to the Sinai in 1982. All three soldiers from the 41st (Field

Artillery) FA are wearing M17A2 protective masks coupled with the M6A2 hood. (PAO24ID)

Above: Command Sergeant-Major Luke and Lieutenant-Colonel Lutz point to their intended objective during Operation Desert Storm in 1991. In readiness for the Iraqis unleashing chemical and biological warfare agents, American soldiers were fitted out in chemical suits, as shown here. (PAO24ID)

Above: O.J. Simpson interviews members of Division Artillery of the 24th Infantry Division during Desert Shield/Storm. The soldiers are wearing the standard BDUs and 'boonie' hats in a desert scheme. The vehicle in the background is a multiple launch rocket system known affectionately as a 'Scud-buster' by the troops. (PAO24ID)

Opposite page: Amidst the wreckage of the Iraqi army in Kuwait, this artilleryman from the 41st FA is armed with a M16A2 rifle mounted with a 40-mm M203 grenade launcher. The soldier is wearing the body armor vest with desert camouflage over his chemical suit with woodland camouflage scheme. (PAO24ID)

Left: Victory in the desert. A soldier from Division Artillery of the 24th Infantry Division places an American flag in the barrel of an Iraqi heavy machine-gun. He is wearing a body armor vest over his olive-green chemical suit. Protruding from his vest is a captured Iraqi AK-47 or AKM bayonet. (PAO24ID)

Above: The personal armor system for Ground Troops (PASGT) Kevlar helmet came into use in 1978, but it was not until 1984 that the M1 helmet was finally discontinued. The Kevlar helmet is commonly referred to as the 'Fritz' because of its similarity to the shape of the World War II German *Stahlhelm*. (PAO24ID)

Left: A specialist four from the 116th FA wearing the woodland pattern BDU constructed of cotton carded rip-stop wind resistant poplin for hot climates, Fort Homer Hesterly, Florida, 2000. He has pinned his metal rank insignia unto the front of his BDU cap. Note the plastic canteen that was adopted during the Vietnam War. (AMQ)

Above: A HMMWV or 'humvee' from the 265th ADA is equipped with a surface-to-air missile system designed to counter the high-speed, low-altitude enemy air threat to forward elements and vital areas. This was photographed at an airshow in MacDill Air Force Base, Florida in April 2000. (AMQ) NOTE THIS IS COLOUR

Below: In 1991 the Desert Storm camouflage scheme – universally known as the chocolate-chip pattern by the GIs who wore it during that campaign – was replaced. An army colonel from Central Command (CENTCOM) in MacDill Air Force Base is seen wearing this new pattern. (AMQ)

A Fl Guardsman from the 116th Field Artillery stands beside the very reliable World War II-vintage 105-mm howitzer M2A1 in April 2000. After a century in finding a reliable, practical, functional, and comfortable uniform for the soldier, the BDU will remain the standard uniform for the armed services of the United States in the years to come. (AMQ)